MYTHICAL BEINGS

ORIGAMI TODAY

MYTHICAL BEINGS

JAY ANSILL
PHOTOGRAPHS BY MARK HILL

HarperPerennial

A Division of HarperCollins*Publishers*

A RUNNING HEADS BOOK

MYTHICAL BEINGS was produced by
Running Heads Incorporated
55 West 21 Street
New York, NY 10010

FIRST EDITION

Editor: Rose K. Phillips
Designer: Liz Trovato
Managing Editor: Jill Hamilton
Production Manager: Peter J. McCulloch

Library of Congress Cataloging-in-Publication Data

Ansill, Jay.
    Mythical beings / Jay Ansill : photographs by Mark Hill.
        p.   cm. —(Origami today : 1)
    Includes bibliographical references
    ISBN 0-06-096866-4 : $10.00
    1. Origami   I. Title.   II. Series.
    TT870.A49   1992
    736'.982—dc20   91-50506
                                                         CIP

Typeset by Trufont Typographers, Inc.
Color separations by Hong Kong Scanner Craft Co., Ltd.
Printed and bound in Hong Kong by C&C Offset Printing Co. Ltd.

92 93 94 95 96 10 9 8 7 6 5 4 3 2 1

DEDICATION

This book is lovingly dedicated to the memory of my mother, Marilynn Ansill.

ACKNOWLEDGMENTS

I wish to thank all of the brilliant and creative folders who have allowed me to include their work in this book. Special thanks to Stephen Weiss for helping me find models and folders. John Montroll was also a big help.

The following people have contributed in one way or another to bringing this book to life, either by helping to make connections, or by lending encouragement, support, and inspiration: Lillian Oppenheimer, Holly Hartzell, Jeanne Fisher, Janel Derstine, the staff of the Friends of the Origami Center of America (in particular Tony Cheng), Dave Venables, Susan Shoenfeld, Dave Brill, Pia and David Ansill, Samuel Randlett, Rolly Brown, Bill Masi, Roberta Tucci, Keonaona Peterson, John Michel, Rose K. Phillips and the staff at Running Heads, and of course Claudia Balant.

CONTENTS

INTRODUCTION

Although paperfolding was first practiced centuries ago, it has been only in the past fifty years or so that the creative aspects of origami were explored in depth. Paperfolding began in China, where paper was first developed. From there it moved to Japan, where origami (from the Japanese *ori*, "to fold," and *kami*, "paper") was used for ceremonial and decorative purposes. Paperfolding is most closely associated today with the Japanese tradition.

The idea of creating origami models was first popularized in the 1940s by the master Akira Yoshizawa, who has created hundreds of lifelike designs. Yoshizawa also helped to develop the system of diagramming that has become the international standard. As his work became known in the West, he influenced a generation of folders, changing what had been a child's pastime into a bonafide art form.

Books by Robert Harbin in the 1960s and 1970s brought origami to a wide audience in Britain and America, and the work of such practitioners as Neal Elias, Ligia Montoya, and Robert Neale became standards in the ever-growing world of origami. Models that would have been thought impossible to make a few years ago are now being produced every day. New ideas and models are circulated worldwide by a growing number of clubs and organizations devoted to origami. Two of the largest are the Friends of the Origami Center of America and the British Origami Society (see Sources, page 95).

The question of creativity in origami, as with any artistic endeavor, is difficult to address. Methods vary with each folder, although there are some common threads which are worth exploring. Many folders first experiment by making little variations in existing models—for example, changing the posture of an animal or the shape of the head can change the character of a model. After a while one notices that it is possible to take the basic folds of one model and make a completely different one by utilizing the points in a different way. Robert Lang's Shiva (page 70) is based on his Praying Mantis. The hind legs of the Praying Mantis are used to make the four arms of Shiva, and Shiva's legs come from the forelegs of the Praying Mantis. Robert Neale's Wizard and Witch (page 25) are variations of each other.

One may make fascinating discoveries by simply "doodling," or improvising. This involves experimenting with paper with no particular object in mind. It is likely that something recognizable will begin to emerge. Then it is simply a matter of making the details. In order to make doodling more productive, it is advisable to learn as many models as possible. This way you will have more techniques at your disposal and solving problems will be easier.

As the ability to solve problems develops, it will become possible to envision a finished model and devise a method of folding it from scratch. The origami artist John Montroll once said that when he is working on a particular subject—for example, fish—he obtains a photographic book and starts from the beginning and works through it, creating versions of everything depicted. To my knowledge, only a few folders have reached this level of dedication and expertise.

It is my hope that by learning the models in this book you will be inspired to create your own.

PART ONE

THE BASICS

PAPER CHOICES

Almost any kind of paper can be used for origami, but to obtain the best results, use a type that is strong enough not to tear, and crisp enough to retain the folds. Most art-supply stores, hobby shops, and many bookstores carry origami paper; that is, paper precut into squares and brightly colored on one side and white on the other. It is advisable to use a large piece of paper for your first attempt, especially for the more complex models.

Foil-backed paper is available as gift wrap and also in precut squares. Many folders prefer to use foil paper as it retains its folds better than ordinary paper, but it has a few drawbacks. Creases often crack and lose strength, and once you make a fold, wrinkle, or even a slight crease, it leaves a permanent mark on the surface of the paper, making it less attractive.

One of the most exciting innovations in paper comes from origami artist Robert Lang. He suggests taking a piece of aluminum foil and, with spray adhesive, attaching tissue paper to both sides. The translucence of the tissue allows the foil to remain slightly visible, giving the paper a frosted and metallic appearance. The texture and flexibility of the paper make the final models more sculptural. The main drawback of this paper is that creases are difficult to reverse. Despite this problem, the most complex models can be made from "tissue foil" and the results can be fantastic. Several of the photographs in this book depict models that were made from tissue foil; Daedalus and Shiva are good examples.

Another relatively recent development is "wet folding." This involves keeping the paper damp with a plant sprayer or cloth while folding. This technique enables you to shape the paper into three-dimensional forms. It has the added benefit of making the finished model more sturdy when it dries. Experiment with different kinds of paper and compare results. I have had success with calligraphy parchment, which is available at art supply stores. The Centaur and Cerberus in this book are examples of the possibilities of wet folding.

A large selection of paper can be ordered from the Friends of the Origami Center of America and the British Origami Society (see Sources, page 95).

BASIC FOLDS, SYMBOLS, AND BASES

An illustrative system of lines, dots, dashes, and arrows has been devised to make the diagrams easier to understand. Most origami books use these symbols, which constitute an international visual language. Although the diagrams that follow are self-explanatory, keep in mind the following principles:

Arrows indicate the direction of a fold.

Dots and dashes are used to indicate the folds themselves.

Dashes alone indicate a concave crease, or valley fold.

Dots alternating with dashes indicate a convex crease, or mountain fold; in this case, the paper is folded over.

Throughout the book, diagrams are shaded to indicate that the colored side of the paper should be facing outward.

Also included in this section are traditional Japanese bases. These are named for ancient models that use them as a starting point. Hundreds of contemporary models are folded from these bases. Like musical scales, they are the stepping stones to creativity and innovation. In many of the introductions to the models, the text will refer to one of these folds or bases as a starting point. Simply turn to this section to find the relevant fold or base, and then resume with the step-by-step directions provided for the particular model.

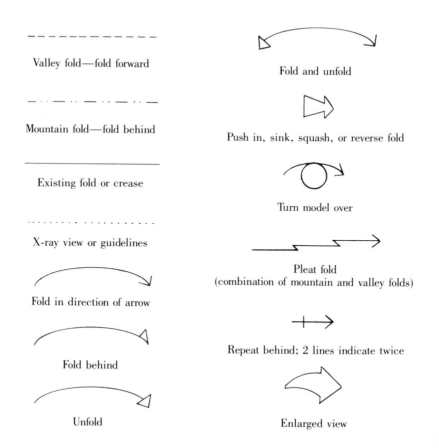

Valley fold—fold forward

Fold and unfold

Mountain fold—fold behind

Push in, sink, squash, or reverse fold

Existing fold or crease

Turn model over

X-ray view or guidelines

Pleat fold
(combination of mountain and valley folds)

Fold in direction of arrow

Repeat behind; 2 lines indicate twice

Fold behind

Unfold

Enlarged view

PRELIMINARY FOLD

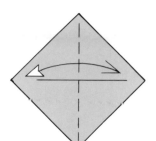

1. Fold and unfold.

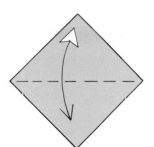

2. Fold and unfold.

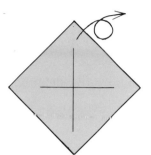

3. Turn over.

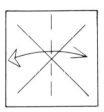

4. Fold and unfold.

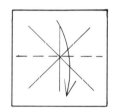

5.

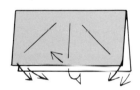

6a. Bring corners together.

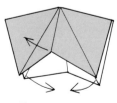

6b.

1–6b.

7. Completed Preliminary Fold.

PETAL FOLD

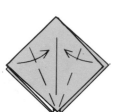

1. Begin with Preliminary Fold.

2.

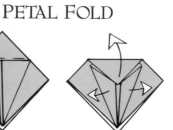

3. Unfold.

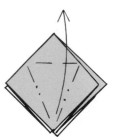

4a. Lift flap as far as it will go.

4b.

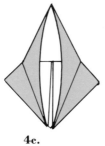

4c.

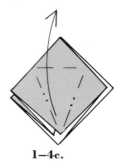

1–4c.

5. Completed Petal Fold.

BIRD BASE

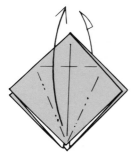

1. Petal fold; repeat behind.

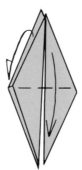

2.

3. Completed Bird Base.

SQUASH FOLD

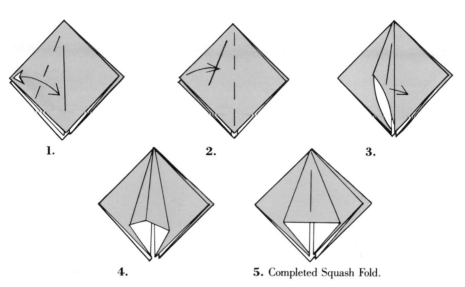

1. **2.** **3.**

4. **5.** Completed Squash Fold.

RABBIT EAR

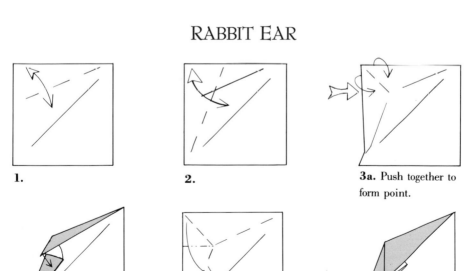

1. **2.** **3a.** Push together to form point.

3b. **1–3b.** **4.** Completed Rabbit Ear.

DOUBLE RABBIT EAR

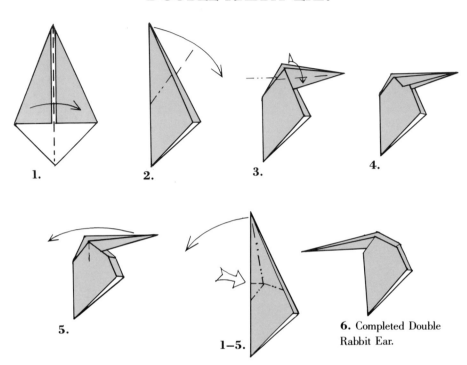

1.

2.

3.

4.

5.

1–5.

6. Completed Double Rabbit Ear.

STRETCH FOLD

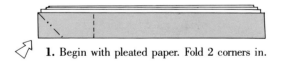

1. Begin with pleated paper. Fold 2 corners in.

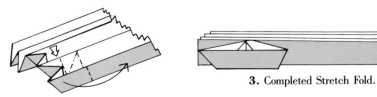

2. Pull as far as it will go.

3. Completed Stretch Fold.

FISH BASE

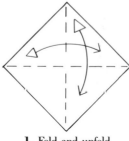

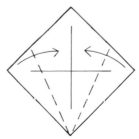

1. Fold and unfold.

2.

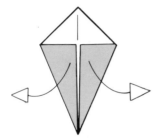

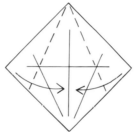

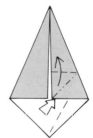

3. Unfold.

4.

5. Squash fold.

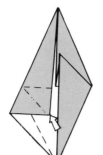

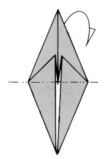

6. Squash fold.

7. Fold behind.

8. Completed
Fish Base.

REVERSE AND CRIMP FOLDS

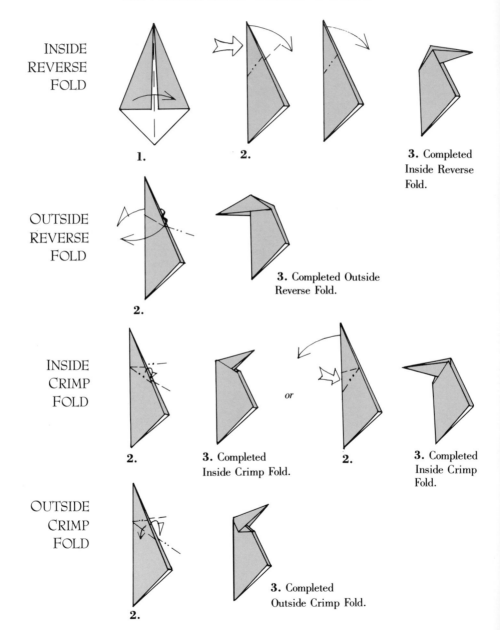

INSIDE
REVERSE
FOLD

1. **2.** **3.** Completed Inside Reverse Fold.

OUTSIDE
REVERSE
FOLD

2. **3.** Completed Outside Reverse Fold.

INSIDE
CRIMP
FOLD

or

2. **3.** Completed Inside Crimp Fold. **2.** **3.** Completed Inside Crimp Fold.

OUTSIDE
CRIMP
FOLD

2. **3.** Completed Outside Crimp Fold.

WATER BOMB BASE

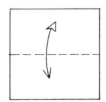

1. Fold and unfold.

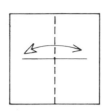

2. Fold and unfold.

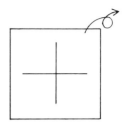

3.

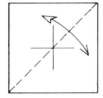

4. Fold and unfold.

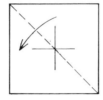

5.

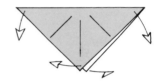

6. Bring horizontal.

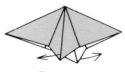

7.

8. Completed Water Bomb Base.

19

PART TWO
THE MODELS

MYTHOLOGY, ART, AND ORIGAMI

Human beings have always searched for meaning in the workings of the universe. The fantastic myths and folk tales of the Greeks, Celts, Native Americans, and other cultures are, on the simplest level, answers to what were at the time inexplicable phenomena. In a much deeper sense, the secrets of these legends and the beings that populate them continue to resonate within us, despite the influences of science and philosophy.

To my way of thinking, the need to express ourselves in artistic terms comes from the same part of our consciousness. For centuries painters, poets, musicians, and other artists have challenged us to discover the story of ourselves, to find the common bonds that link us to each other and to our past. This is the role of the artist in society, and not one to be taken lightly.

As an art form, origami is unique in the limitations placed on the artist. It combines a sense of geometry and engineering with an artistic eye and more than a little dexterity. Origami is in one sense a game, a contest between the folder and the square. But hidden not too deep inside these creases is the simple secret that says a great deal about the structure of our universe and ourselves.

The models that follow represent some of the most magnificent mythical creatures imagined by a variety of cultures. Dragons are an especially popular motif, and they take on several intriguing forms in this book. Advanced students of origami should find them challenging to create, while novices may want to make the models in the order they are presented in the book—which runs from easiest to most difficult. Rated on a scale of difficulty from 1 to 4, the following would apply: Ouroboros, 1; Wizard and Witch, 2; Winged Dragon, 3; Gargoyle, 3; Daedalus, 3; Pegasus, 3; Flapping Dragon, 3; Woodland Elf, 3; Centaur, 3; Rearing Dragon, 3; Shiva, 4; Unicorn, 4; Long-Tailed Dragon, 4; and Cerberus, 4.

Whatever your level of expertise, creating these mythical origami creatures should prove to be an absorbing and fulfilling experience.

OUROBOROS

The worm eating its tail is a symbolic creature with ancient Egyptian and
Greek origins. It was mainly used by the gnostics to represent, broadly
speaking, the eternal cycle of life. It also symbolizes completion and
perfection. Ouroboros is sometimes depicted half dark and half light. In
this sense it is similar to the Chinese yin-yang symbol of counterbalanc-
ing opposing principles. I have developed a variation of Robert Neale's
model to achieve the two-colored effect. The model looks best when the
tip of the tail is touching the head and the crimp folds give the tail and
neck a circular look.

1. Begin with fish base.

2. Fold back and rotate.

3. Fold and unfold. Repeat behind.

4. Squash fold.

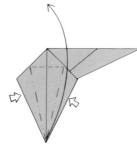

5. Petal fold.

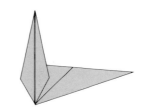

6. Repeat steps 4–5 behind.

7. Valley fold front flap only and rotate.

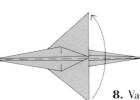

8. Valley fold.

9. Alternate: Pull out one layer to change color.

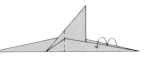

9a. Valley fold.

23

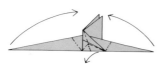

10a. Reverse fold both sides.
  b. Rabbit ear. Repeat behind.

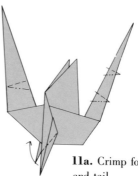

11a. Crimp fold neck
and tail.
  b. Reverse fold foot.
  Repeat behind.

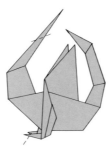

12. Reverse fold neck.
Reverse fold feet. Repeat behind.

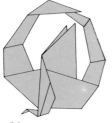

13a. Pull out loose
paper from inside.
Repeat behind.

13b. Reverse fold.

13.

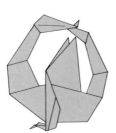

14. Body should suggest circle.
Completed Ouroborus.

24

WIZARD AND WITCH

Origami artist Robert Neale has the gift of being able to express a great deal in simple terms. Simplicity is, after all, at the heart of the concept of origami. In these models, such details as arms and legs are only suggested and the heads are exaggerated, but all this seems to accentuate their charm. These are neither the witches of *Macbeth* stirring the cauldron, nor Merlin of Arthurian legend; instead, these little gems resemble children in Halloween costumes.

WIZARD

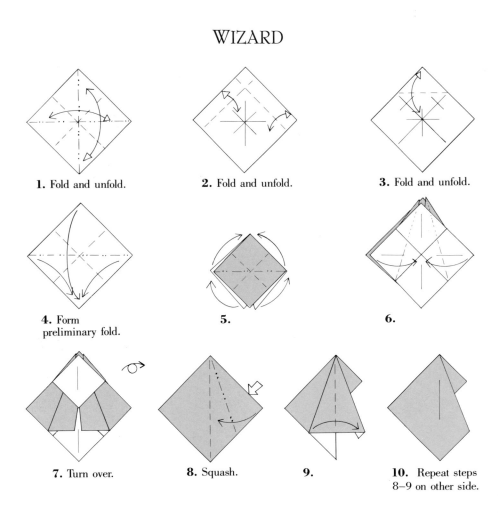

1. Fold and unfold.

2. Fold and unfold.

3. Fold and unfold.

4. Form preliminary fold.

5.

6.

7. Turn over.

8. Squash.

9.

10. Repeat steps 8–9 on other side.

11. Turn over.

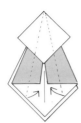

12.

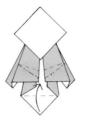

13. Crimp fold.
Crimp fold.
Fold under flap.

14.

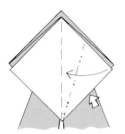

14a. Squash fold head.

15.

16. Repeat steps 14–15
on other side.

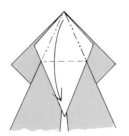

17. Petal fold.

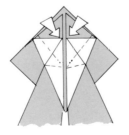

18. Squash fold both sides.

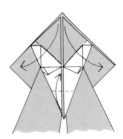

19.

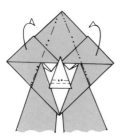

20. Tuck inside pocket on both sides. Crimp fold nose.

21. Crease nose to make 3-D.

21a. Squash fold both sides of nose.

22. Make model 3-D by creasing along lines.

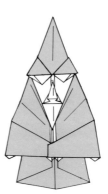

23. Completed Wizard.

WITCH

Follow steps 1–6 for Wizard.

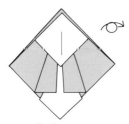 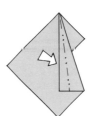

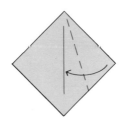

7. Turn over.

8.

9. Squash fold.

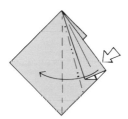 

10. Squash.

11.

12. Repeat steps 9–11 on other side.

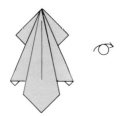

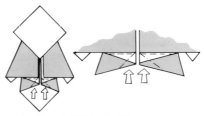

13. Turn over.

14. Squash fold both sides.
Follow steps 14–19 of Wizard for head.

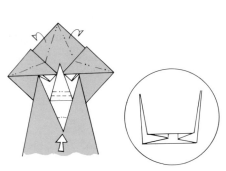 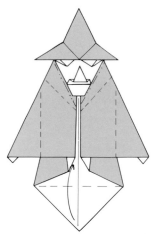

15. Tuck inside flap on both sides.
Crimp fold nose.
Close-up of sink fold.

16. Crease nose to make 3-D
as in Wizard step 21.
Crease along fold lines.
Tuck inside.

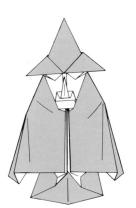

17. Completed Witch.

WINGED DRAGON

Another creation by Robert Neale, this Winged Dragon is a contemporary classic, with all the charm of a traditional model. I have found that altering the placement of the crimp folds in the neck and tail can actually change this dragon's character. This is probably my all-time favorite fold. It is a perfect example of what is enjoyable about origami.

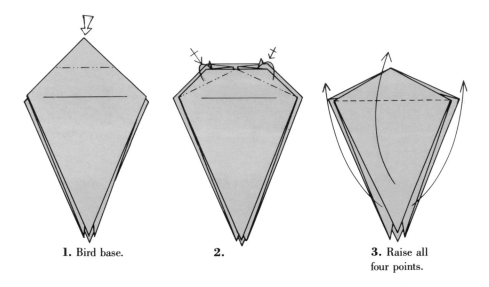

1. Bird base.

2.

3. Raise all
four points.

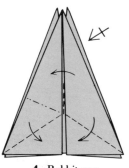

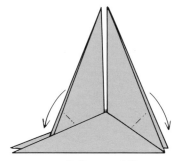

4. Rabbit ear.
Repeat behind.

5. Reverse fold.

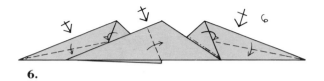

6.

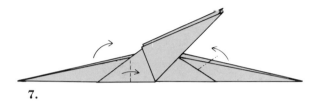

7.

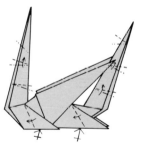

8. Crimp neck and tail.

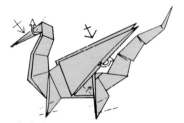

9. Lift one layer of the head.
Repeat behind.

10.

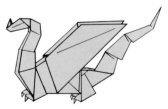

11. Completed Winged Dragon.

GARGOYLE

Gargoyles are fantastic creatures of human or animal form. Originally, they were carved stone figures meant to frighten evil spirits away from churches. Today, they are often seen protruding not only from churches, but from older buildings of all kinds. Gargoyles are often as humorous as they are frightening. This creation by Jerry Harris is not unlike the monsters carved in stone. A funny-looking and slightly menacing beast, it is also a clever piece of origami, utilizing the rarely used blintzed frog base as a starting point.

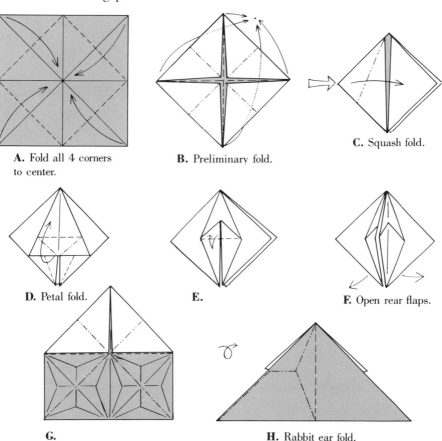

A. Fold all 4 corners to center.

B. Preliminary fold.

C. Squash fold.

D. Petal fold.

E.

F. Open rear flaps.

G.

H. Rabbit ear fold.

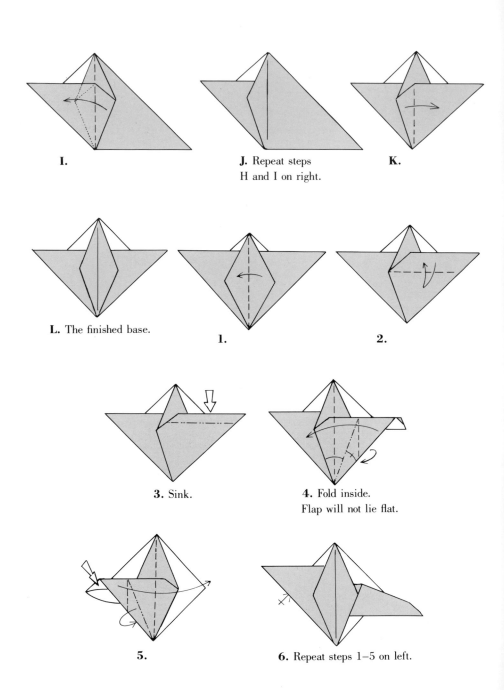

I.

J. Repeat steps
H and I on right.

K.

L. The finished base.

1.

2.

3. Sink.

4. Fold inside.
Flap will not lie flat.

5.

6. Repeat steps 1–5 on left.

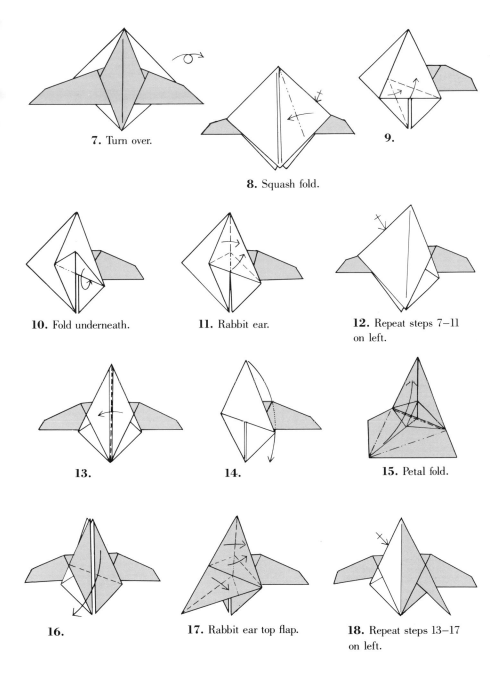

7. Turn over.

8. Squash fold.

9.

10. Fold underneath.

11. Rabbit ear.

12. Repeat steps 7–11 on left.

13.

14.

15. Petal fold.

16.

17. Rabbit ear top flap.

18. Repeat steps 13–17 on left.

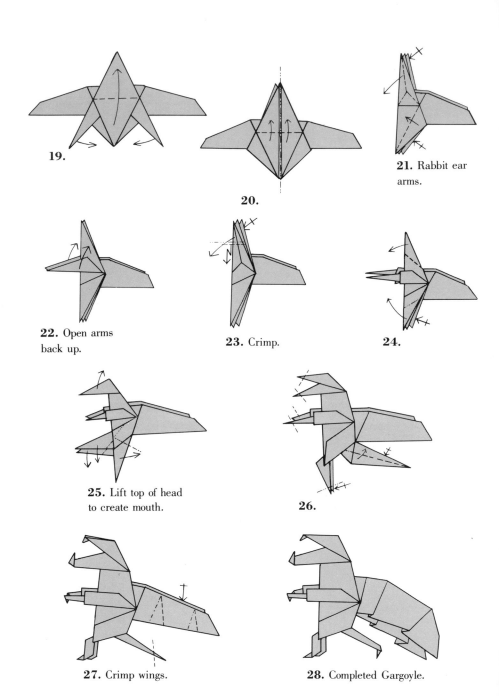

19.

20.

21. Rabbit ear arms.

22. Open arms back up.

23. Crimp.

24.

25. Lift top of head to create mouth.

26.

27. Crimp wings.

28. Completed Gargoyle.

DAEDALUS

Daedalus was a highly skilled builder, renowned for building the labyrinth for King Minos on the island of Crete. After losing favor with the king, Daedalus was imprisoned in a tower and decided that the best way to escape was to fly. He made a pair of wings for himself and a pair for his son Icarus. During the flight, Icarus flew too close to the sun, melting the wax that held the wings together, and fell into the sea and drowned. Daedalus flew to safety in Sicily. Gabriel Alvarez's Daedalus model is one of the most graceful and natural in all origami.

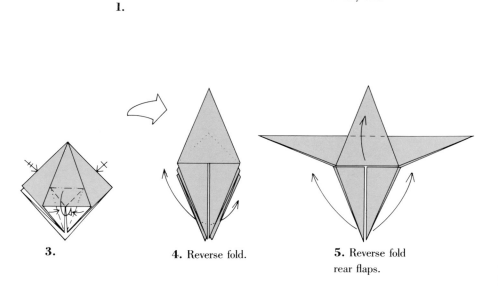

1.

2. Preliminary fold.

3.

4. Reverse fold.

5. Reverse fold rear flaps.

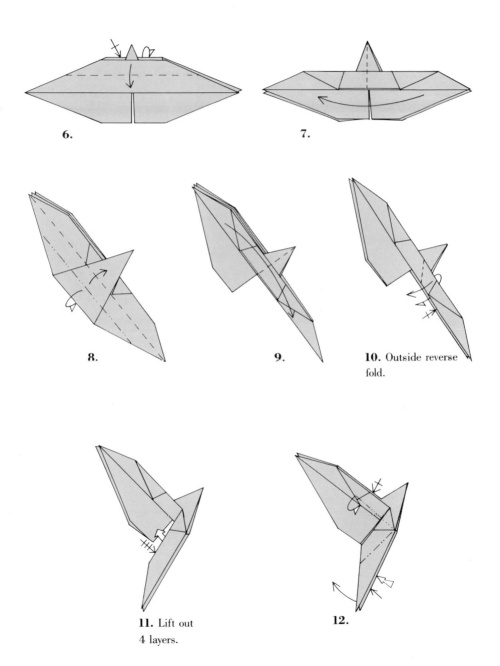

6.

7.

8.

9.

10. Outside reverse fold.

11. Lift out 4 layers.

12.

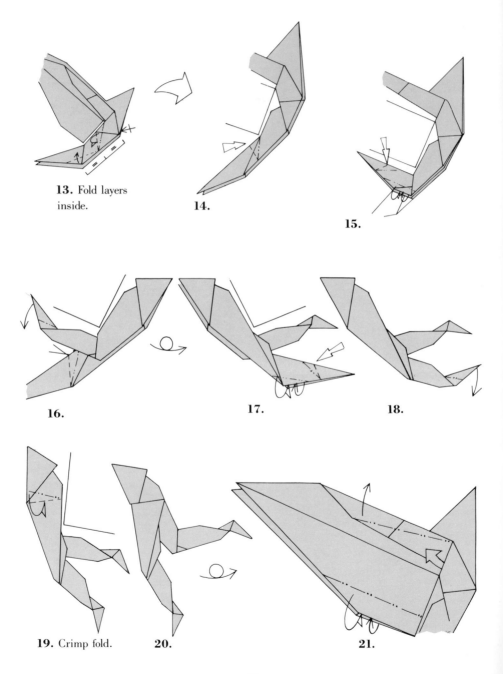

13. Fold layers inside.

14.

15.

16.

17.

18.

19. Crimp fold.

20.

21.

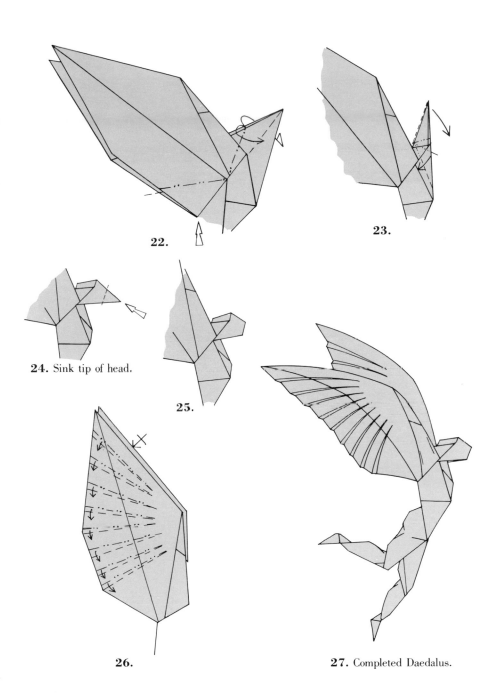

22.

23.

24. Sink tip of head.

25.

26.

27. Completed Daedalus.

43

PEGASUS

The winged horse is one of the most well-known figures of Greek mythology. Pegasus sprang fully formed from the body of Medusa the Gorgon, who was slain by Perseus. The fountain of Hippocrene on the Muses' mountain of Helicon was opened with a kick from his hoof. Many folders have tried their hands at Pegasus. The one presented here was created by Gabriel Alvarez and begins, like many of the others, with a blintzed bird base. The base provides the correct number of points to form the head, tail, legs, and wings. Alvarez has captured the beauty and stature of this gentle creature.

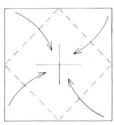

1. Fold 4 corners to center.

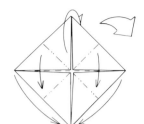

2. Preliminary fold.

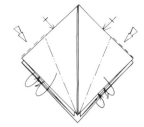

3.

4. Pull out loose flaps.

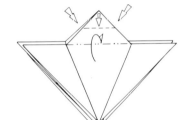

5. Partial sink.

6. Lift middle flaps.

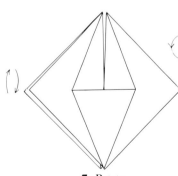

7. Rotate.

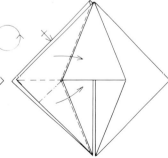

8. Rabbit ear. Repeat.

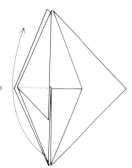

9.

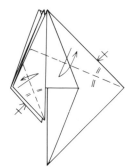

10.

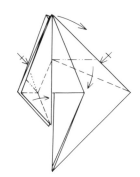

11. Rabbit ear flaps on left.

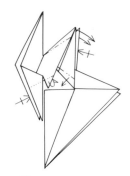

12.

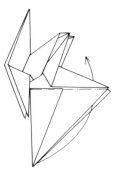

13.

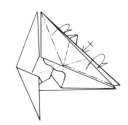

14. Fold inside.

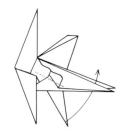

15.

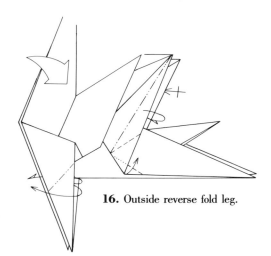

16. Outside reverse fold leg.

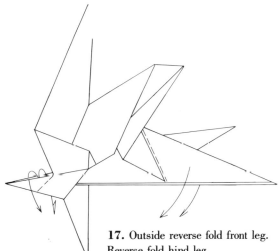

17. Outside reverse fold front leg.
Reverse fold hind leg.

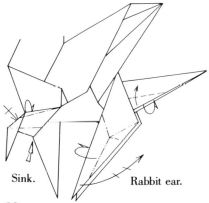

Sink.

Rabbit ear.

18.

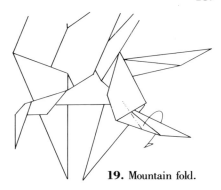

19. Mountain fold.

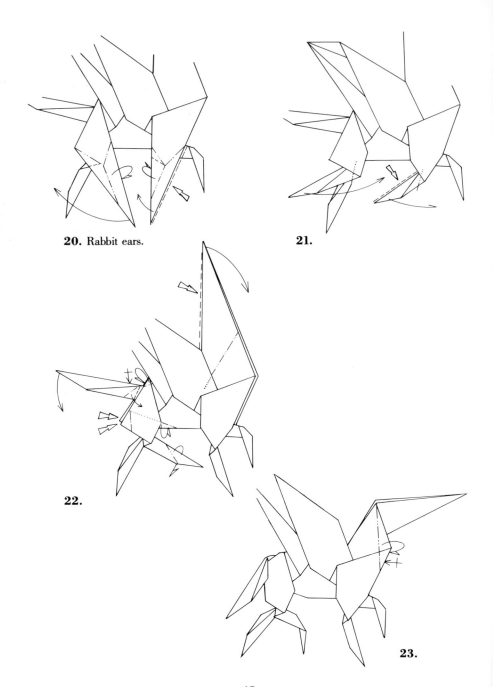

20. Rabbit ears.

21.

22.

23.

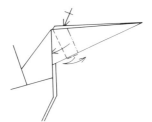

24. Crimp fold.

25. Outside reverse fold.

26. Pull out layers.

27.

28. Shape head.

29. Completed Pegasus.

FLAPPING DRAGON

One of Stephen Weiss's specialties is coming up with figures that reflect the whimsical side of origami. Some of the most humorous pieces are the ones that can be made to actually do something. When this dragon is grasped at the bottom of the tail and lower neck and gently pushed a bit toward the middle, its wings will flap!

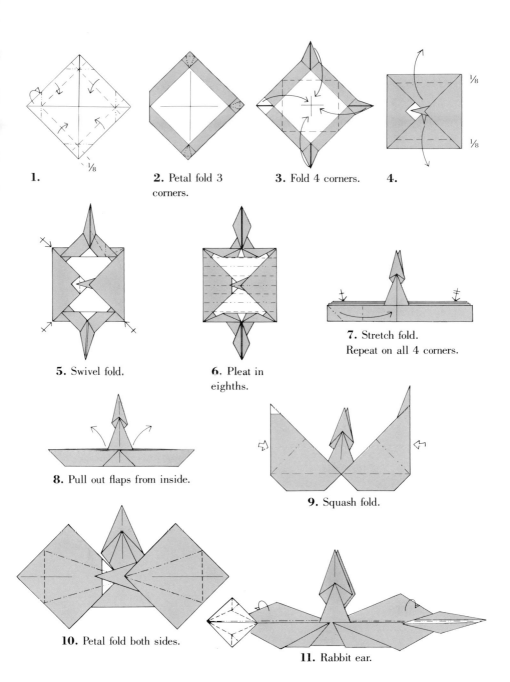

1.   ⅛

2. Petal fold 3 corners.

3. Fold 4 corners.

4.   ⅛   ⅛

5. Swivel fold.

6. Pleat in eighths.

7. Stretch fold. Repeat on all 4 corners.

8. Pull out flaps from inside.

9. Squash fold.

10. Petal fold both sides.

11. Rabbit ear.

51

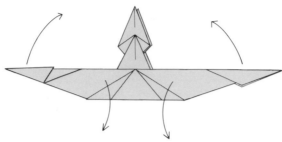

12. Pull both flaps on left.
Mountain fold outer points up;
this will bring inner points down.

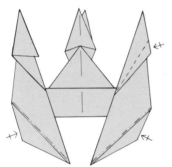

13. Mountain fold.
Repeat behind.

13a. Detail of inside
of wing. Crimp fold.
Repeat on opposite
wing.

13b. Tuck under flap
on other side. Repeat
on opposite wing.

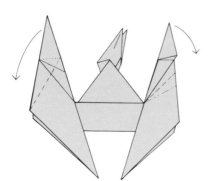

14.

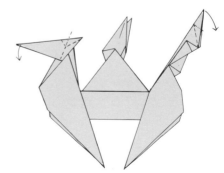

15. Rabbit ear. Pull bottom jaw.

15a. Outside reverse fold.

15b.

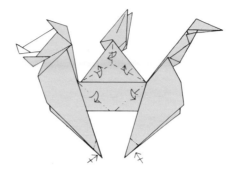

16. Reverse fold foot. Repeat on all 4 legs. Crease as shown.

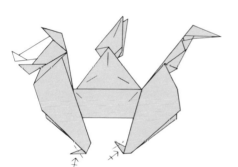

17. Reverse fold foot. Repeat on all 4 legs.

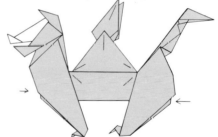

18. Completed Flapping Dragon. Push in at arrows to make wings flap.

WOODLAND ELF

This clever model, created by Stephen Weiss, is a good example of using pleated paper—a technique pioneered by Neal Elias. The use of pleated paper has opened up new possibilities in designing origami figures, although the proportions of certain models may require the use of rectangular paper. Here the arms and legs of the elf are stretched from the pleated base. Even today, people still believe in the "little people." When an old woman from Galway was asked if she believed in elves or leprechauns, she replied firmly, "No, but they're out there!"

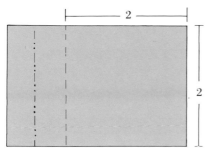

1. Use 2 × 3 rectangle, color side up.

2. Pleat in sixteenths. Crease.

3. Pull single layer up 90° to long portion. Each pleat must be swiveled up and back on corresponding long pleat below it. Work back and forth from bottom to top, moving layer up a little at a time.

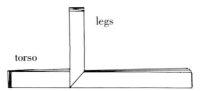

legs

torso

4. Starting from the third corner bottom on each side of leg pleats, stretch the pleats to separate the legs. Note that stretching brings all folded edges up even on top and the layer of the center will rise up from the bottom to allow this at the middle folded edge.

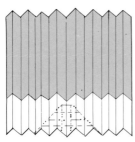

4a. Excess paper around the crotch is pushed in to wrap around vertical center edge of body as best it can.

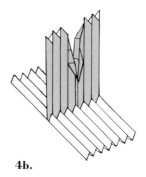

4b.

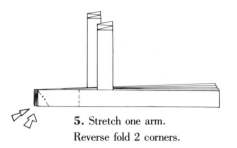

5. Stretch one arm.
Reverse fold 2 corners.

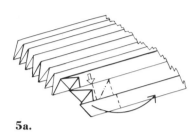

5a.

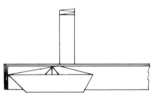

5b. Repeat behind.

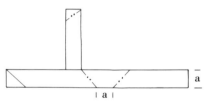

$| \ a \ |$

6. Make 2 ordered 90° reverse folds with layers even on both sides. Note that the distance (a) between reverses equals the width of one pleat.

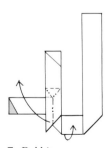

7. Rabbit ear arm.
Repeat behind. Color change base by wrapping a single layer to the outside on each side. Then open base out flat.

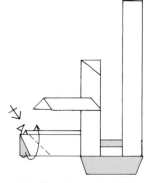

8. Outside reverse fold.

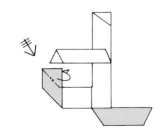

9. Mountain fold all 4.

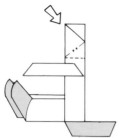

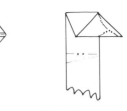

10a.

10. Open up head
so it lies flat.

10b. Valley fold
and fold bottom
layer up inside.

10c. Crimp neck and
round head to make
3-D. Softly rabbit ear
back of hat.

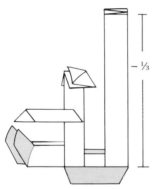

− ⅓

11. Spread mushroom cap from
about ⅓-way from top of pleats
to top of base.

12. Valley fold.

13. Mountain fold.

14. Hook interlocking flaps
to complete mushroom cap.

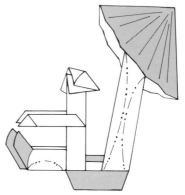

15. Mountain fold joint to lock. Mountain fold edges to round out mushroom, fold corners underneath.

16. Round out mushroom stem and legs.

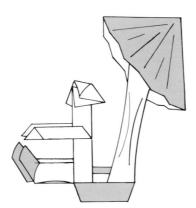

17. Completed Woodland Elf.

CENTAUR

A centaur has the upper body of a human and the lower body of a horse. Cheiron, the most famous centaur, was the instructor of Achilles and other distinguished legendary Greek heroes. Cheiron is seen in the night sky as Sagittarius, the Archer. Neal Elias's interpretation of the centaur is quite ingenious. It is made from 2×1 rectangle.

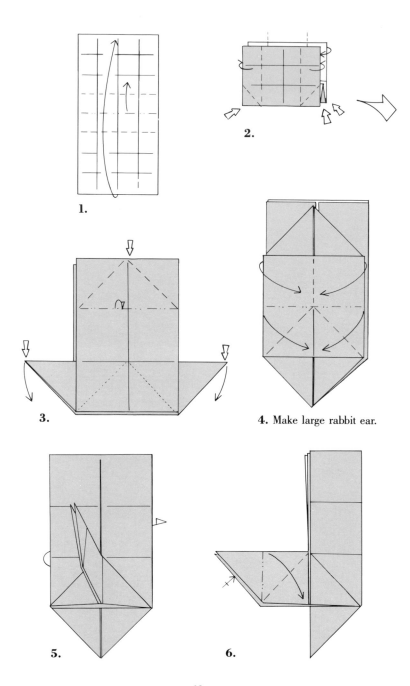

1.

2.

3.

4. Make large rabbit ear.

5.

6.

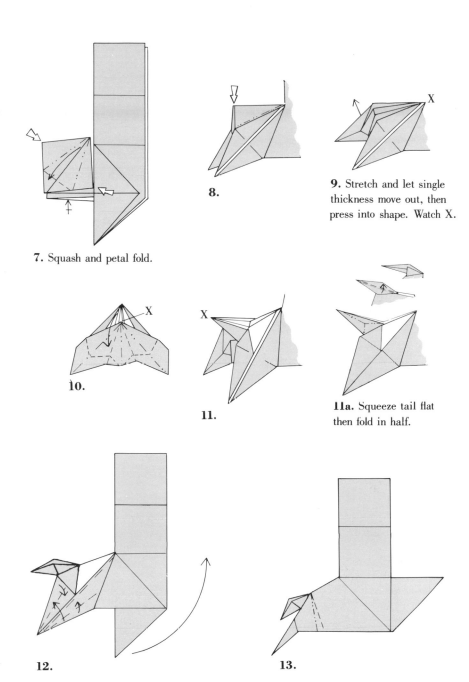

7. Squash and petal fold.

8.

9. Stretch and let single thickness move out, then press into shape. Watch X.

10.

11.

11a. Squeeze tail flat then fold in half.

12.

13.

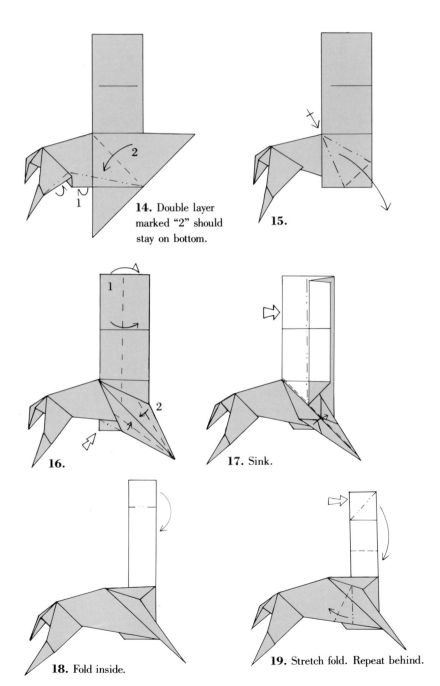

14. Double layer marked "2" should stay on bottom.

15.

16.

17. Sink.

18. Fold inside.

19. Stretch fold. Repeat behind.

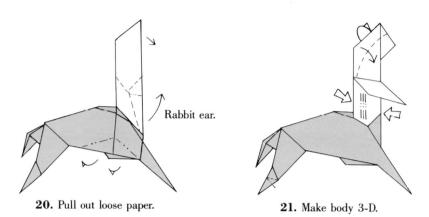

Rabbit ear.

20. Pull out loose paper.

21. Make body 3-D.

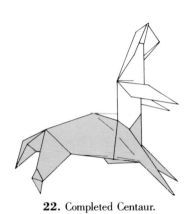

22. Completed Centaur.

REARING DRAGON

This model by Marc Kirschenbaum is a variation on Robert Neale's Winged Dragon. The Rearing Dragon has more detail, however, especially in the head. The mouth opens menacingly, and its remarkably sinister-looking eyes are formed from the reverse side of the paper. Kirschenbaum has created several very complex and imaginative models, all of which carry his distinctive stamp.

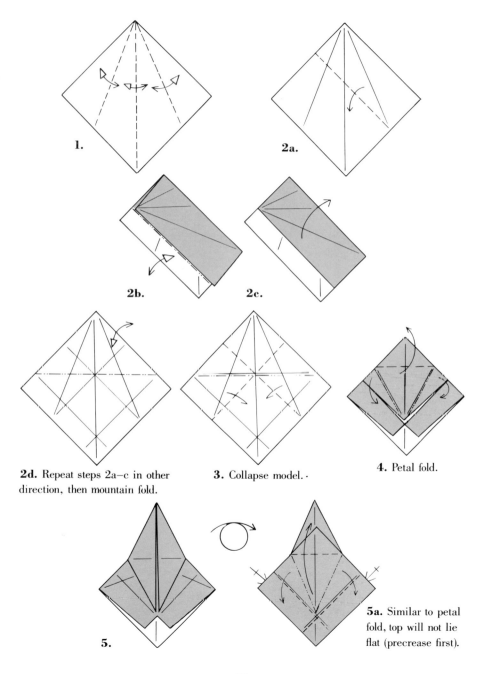

1.

2a.

2b.

2c.

2d. Repeat steps 2a–c in other direction, then mountain fold.

3. Collapse model. ·

4. Petal fold.

5.

5a. Similar to petal fold, top will not lie flat (precrease first).

 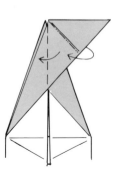

6. Flatten top.

7. Squash fold.

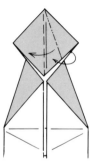 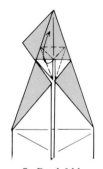 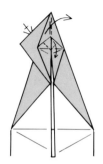

8. Squash fold.

9. Petal fold.

10. Fold over while reverse folding small flap at 45°. Repeat steps 8–10 on other side.

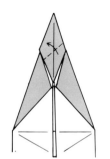 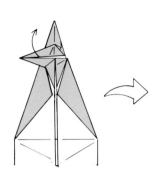 

11. Valley fold lightly.

12. Raise a layer.

13. Mountain fold corner. This will result in a color change at top of small flap.

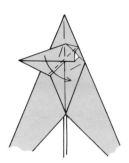

14. Return flap to position in step 11. Repeat steps 11–13 on other side.

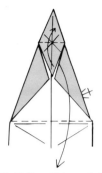

15. Valley fold small flap up and valley|fold large flap down. Repeat behind.

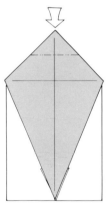

16. Sink top.

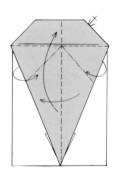

17. Fold in half while simultaneously bringing flap up. Repeat on other side.

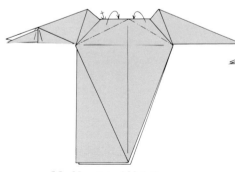

18. Mountain fold 4 times.

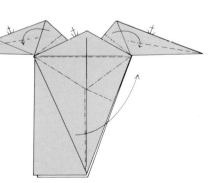

19. Fold sides of tail and neck in rabbit ear wings.

67

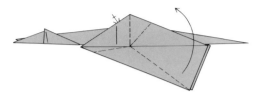

20. Swing wings upwards.

21. Valley fold up a layer of the triangle while pulling out a layer from the wings. Note: the wing must lie perpendicular to the bottom.

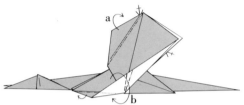

22. Note that (a) and (b) must be folded simultaneously.

22a. Back of wing.

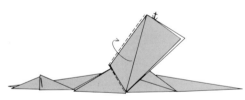

23. Wrap layers around wings.

24. Swing tail into position while valley folding hind legs, rabbit ear front legs.

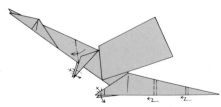

25. Reverse fold neck and flatten head. Crimp tail and round out feet and tail.

27.

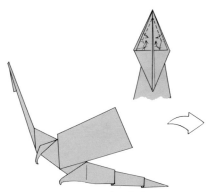

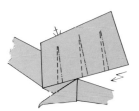

26. Bottom of head: form jaws so as to reveal the eyes and fold in sides of jaws.

27a. Top of head: shape head and neck.

28. Crimp while curling wings.

29. Shape wings by using reverse fold.

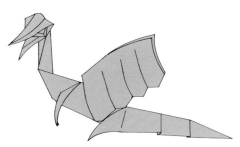

30. Completed Rearing Dragon.

SHIVA

Shiva, the Hindu god known as "the Destroyer," is shown here in the guise of Nataraja, Lord of the Dance. This beautiful work by Robert Lang is quite a challenge to fold, particularly in the shaping of the arms and legs. But this is what gives the figure its distinctively Indian character. Lang has proven here that practically anything can be folded from a square of paper.

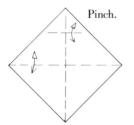

1. White side up; fold and unfold.

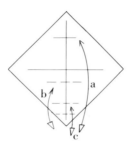

1a. Pinch only.

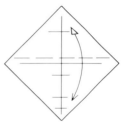

2. Fold and unfold all the way across.

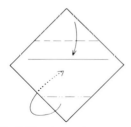

3. Fold points to last crease.

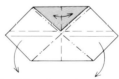

4. Make a hybrid preliminary fold/water bomb base.

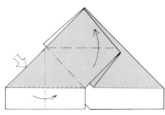

5.

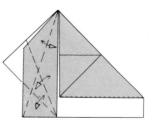

6. Crease angle bisectors.

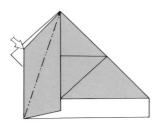

7. Open sink.

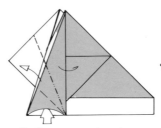

8. Open out and push up paper from the inside.

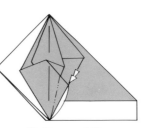

9. Reverse fold.

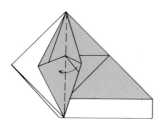

10. Close up.

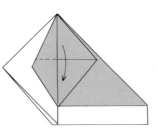

11.

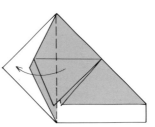

12. Repeat steps 5–12 on right.

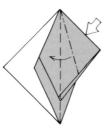

13. Squash fold.

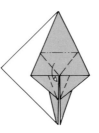

14. Inside petal fold.

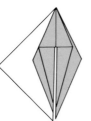

15.

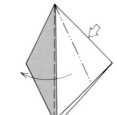

16.

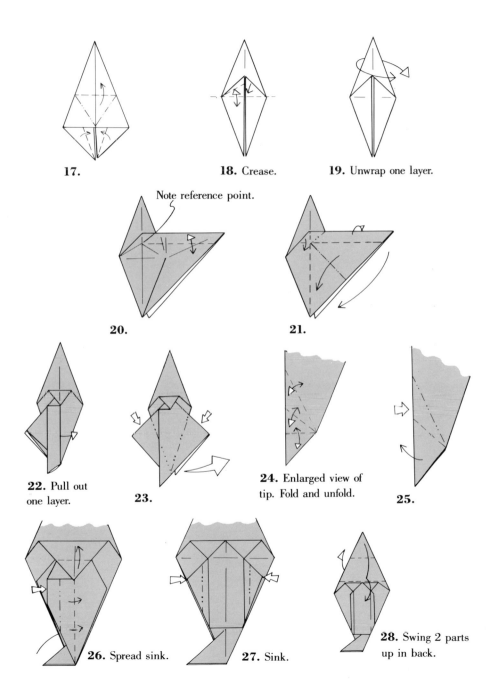

17.

18. Crease.

19. Unwrap one layer.

Note reference point.

20.

21.

22. Pull out one layer.

23.

24. Enlarged view of tip. Fold and unfold.

25.

26. Spread sink.

27. Sink.

28. Swing 2 parts up in back.

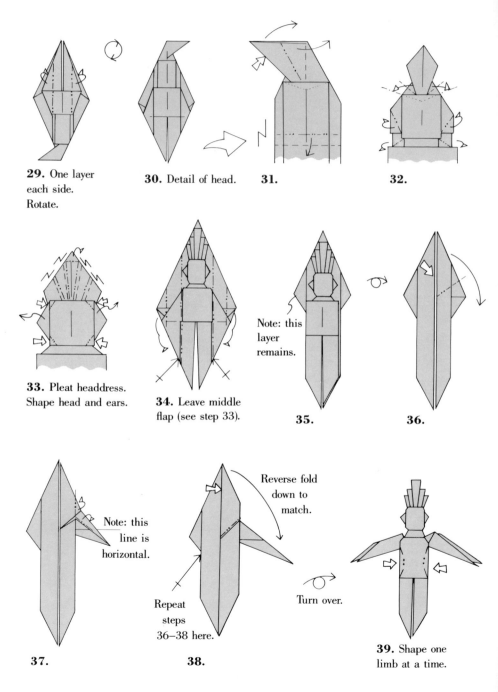

29. One layer each side. Rotate.

30. Detail of head.

31.

32.

33. Pleat headdress. Shape head and ears.

34. Leave middle flap (see step 33).

Note: this layer remains.

35.

36.

Note: this line is horizontal.

37.

Reverse fold down to match.

Repeat steps 36–38 here.

Turn over.

38.

39. Shape one limb at a time.

74

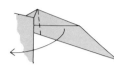

40. Front arm, right side of model (Shiva's left).

41. Outside reverse fold.

42. Narrow and round arm. Sink tip of hand.

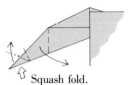

Squash fold.

43. Left front arm.

44. Round arm. Sink tip.

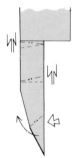

45. Left leg.

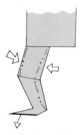

46. Round leg. Open at foot.

47. Right leg.

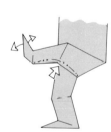

48. Round leg. Open at foot.

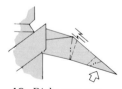

49. Right rear arm.

50. Shape.

51. Repeat steps 49–50 on left, except *curl* hand.

52. Completed Shiva.

75

UNICORN

The unicorn is well known as the gentlest, loveliest beast in legend. Artists' depictions have varied from goat-like to horse-like in nature. Stephen Weiss has created a model that depends on equine features to give grace and power to this horned wonder.

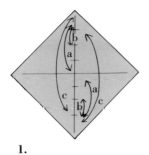

1.

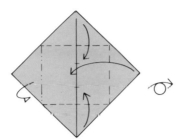

2. By folding the top and bottom corners to the creases made in step 1, the paper forms a 7 × 9 rectangle.

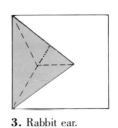

3. Rabbit ear.

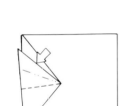

4. Squash fold tip.

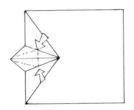

5. Petal fold.

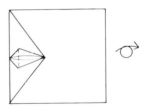

6. Valley fold.

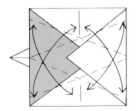

7. Fold corner to meet crease.

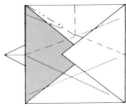

8.

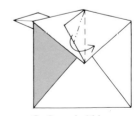

9. Squash fold.

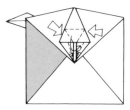

10. Inside petal fold flap.

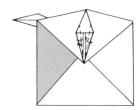

11. Crease.

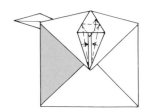

12. Using crease as a guide, petal fold, raising horizontal folded edge while folding sides in.

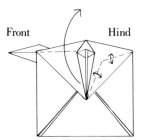

Front   Hind

13. Valley fold front leg up crease, angle bisector on hind leg.

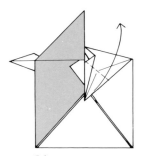

14.

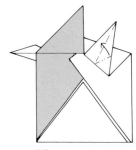

15.

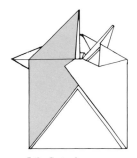

16. Swivel.

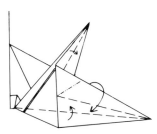

16a.

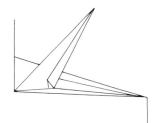

17. Repeat steps 8–16 on bottom.

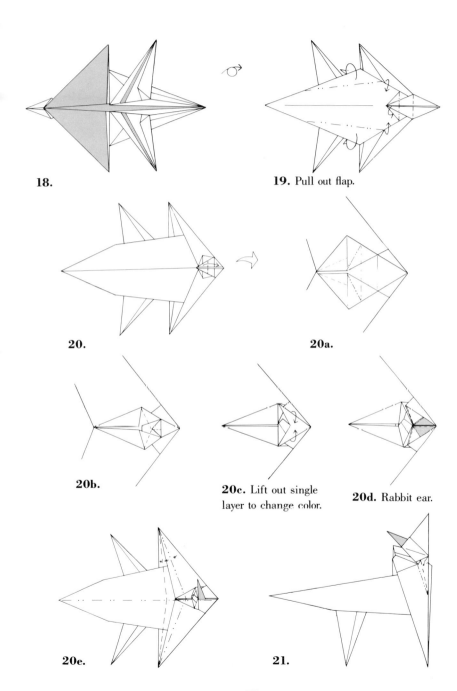

18.

19. Pull out flap.

20.

20a.

20b.

20c. Lift out single layer to change color.

20d. Rabbit ear.

20e.

21.

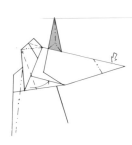

21a. Crease mane. Tuck under flap.
Double rabbit ear to round out horn.

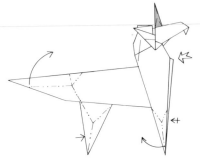

22. Rabbit ear repeat behind.
Sink breast. Double rabbit ear.
Repeat behind so leg points to the right.

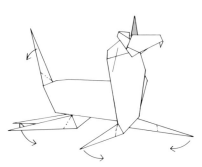

23. Mountain fold, repeat behind.

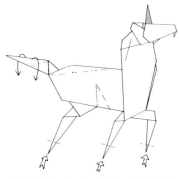

24. Crimp body. Make body 3-D.

24a. Squash.
Repeat on all
4 legs.

24b. Completed
hoof.

25. Completed Unicorn.

Long-Tailed Dragon

Matthew Green's dragon requires a good deal of patience, but the result will prove worthwhile. This dragon is of the winged lizard variety, with its thin body and long tail. This model requires foil paper in order to retain the folds and shape the figure.

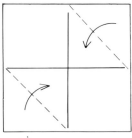

1. Color side up, precreased for Water Bomb Base.

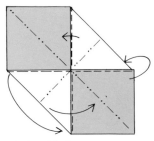

2. Refold along precrease as shown.

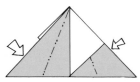

3. Squash fold front and back large points.

4. Fold up the bottom triangle; repeat behind.

5. Fold the corner of the left half of the top flap to the right, so that its bottom edge lines up with the white flap 2 layers beneath.

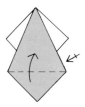

6. Fold the point back to the right, creasing along the vertical center crease of the model.

7. Fold the point's left edge to the center crease.

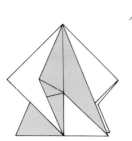

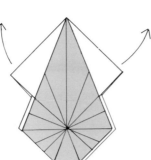

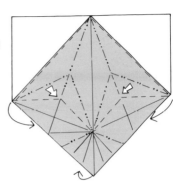

8. Repeat steps 5–7 on right, then on the back 2 flaps. Unfold.

9. Pull out the white corners to reveal all of the new creases.

10. Assemble as shown, both front and back.

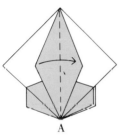

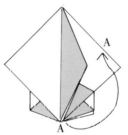

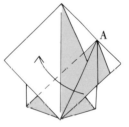

11. Fold the colored portion of the front in half.

12. Reverse fold up the point A.

13. Open up the top flap to reveal the corner of the paper.

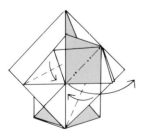

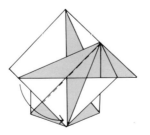

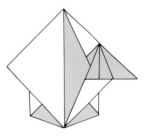

14. Form a rabbit ear fold by pinching and lifting the colored corner and folding in the edges along the precreases.

15. Fold the flap closed again.

16. Repeat steps 11–15 on the back.

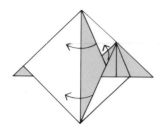

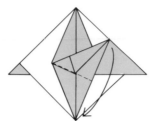

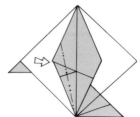

17. Pull one layer only from the right to the left, spreading open some inside creases.

18. Fold the whole flap down to the bottom.

19. Sink fold to narrow the left side.

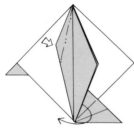

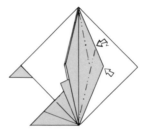

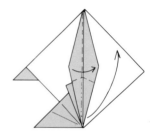

20. Again, sink then reverse fold the 2 inner layers and the pointed flap all the way to the left.

21. Repeat the two sinks on the right.

22. Fold the left half to the right, rotating up the triangular flap at the same time.

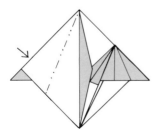

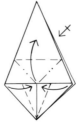

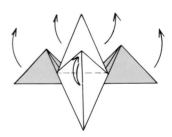

23. Repeat steps 17–22 on the back. Then, squash fold the white flaps.

24. Petal fold, front and back (only white portions shown here).

25. Fold the triangle on the center down and up again. Then, open up the white by pulling out the colored points on the sides.

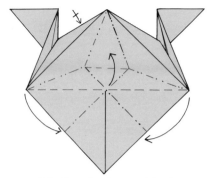

26. Form the front and back opened sections into half bird bases.

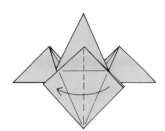

27. Fold the top right flap over to the left.

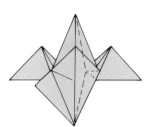

28. Rabbit ear fold the right flap, then undo and fold the flap to the left.

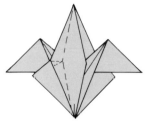

29. Repeat the rabbit ear along the same creases, reversing them, then undo.

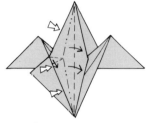

30. Perform a double rabbit ear, one on each layer of the top flap. At the same time, spread the flap open. You may need to reach inside.

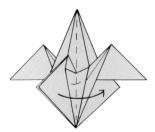

31. Fold 2 layers from the left to the right.

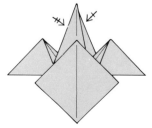

32. Repeat steps 27–31 on the left, then on remaining sides.

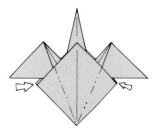

33. Reverse the sides in.

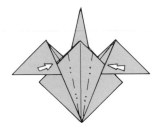

34. Sink to narrow on the left and right.

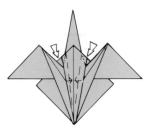

35. Fold the top edges into the middle and squash triangle.

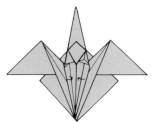

36. Fold the small edges, revealed in step 35, into the center.

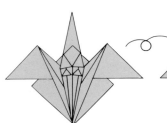

37. Turn over.

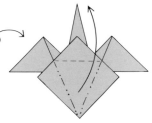

38. Petal fold the top flap.

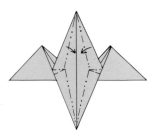

39. Narrow the left and right flaps as in steps 28–30.

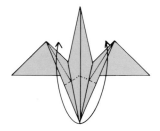

40. Reverse fold the top point from the bottom at the left and right so that the points are a bit inside of the top corner of the wings.

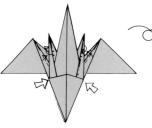

41. Narrow the points by reversing the extra width in, then turn the whole thing over.

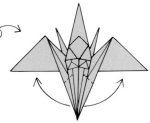

42. Reverse fold out the 2 hind legs.

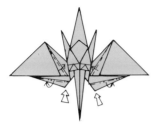

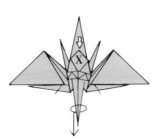

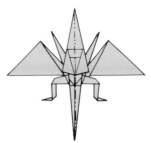

43. Thin out the legs by reversing in the extra width.

44. Reverse fold the legs down, then reverse fold out feet. Pull the tail down spreading point X.

45. Mountain fold the figure in half down the middle and fold the wings up, on a crease right next to the body. There are many layers in the body, so this can be difficult.

46. Reverse fold out front legs and feet. Also, double reverse fold the neck backwards and double crimp out a jaw.

47. Fold the wings loosely along the existing creases. Form head.

48. Completed Long-Tailed Dragon.

CERBERUS

Cerberus, the fierce three-headed dog, guarded the gates to Tartarus, the underworld kingdom of Hades and Persephone. He kept living mortals from entering and prevented ghosts from escaping.

Robert Lang adds his characteristic detailed touch to this Cerberus model. To create it, he took John Montroll's "dog base" and devised a way of giving it three heads.

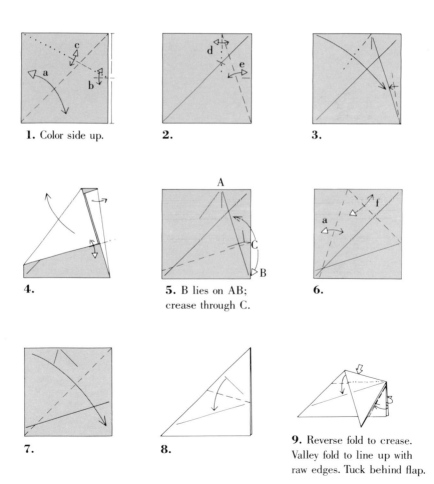

1. Color side up.

2.

3.

4.

5. B lies on AB; crease through C.

6.

7.

8.

9. Reverse fold to crease. Valley fold to line up with raw edges. Tuck behind flap.

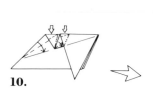

10.

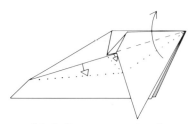

11. Pull out paper and make symmetric. Swing flap up.

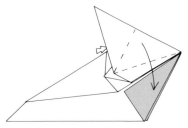

12. Squash fold.

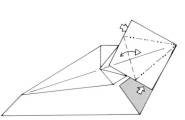

13. Petal fold and unfold.

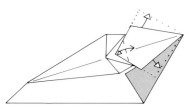

14. Crease, then unfold to 13.

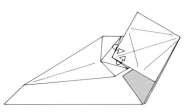

15. Tuck underneath. You have to open out the model to do this.

Turn inside out here.

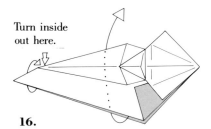

16.

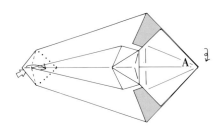

17. Squash fold and turn over.

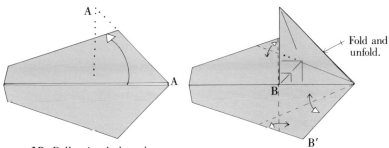

18. Pull point A through
as far as possible.

19. B comes to B'.

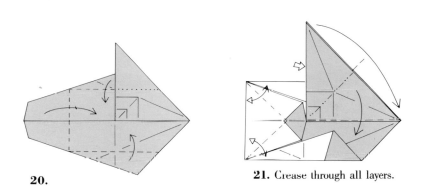

20.

21. Crease through all layers.

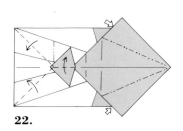

22.

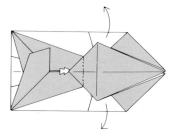

23. Sink on existing creases. Unfold.

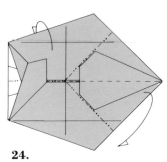

24.

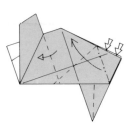

25.

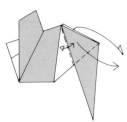

26.

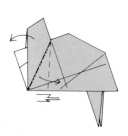

27.

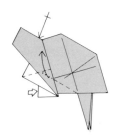

28.

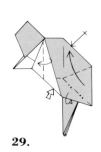

29.

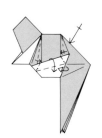

30.

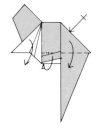

31.

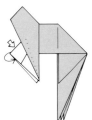

32.

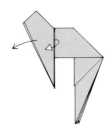

33.

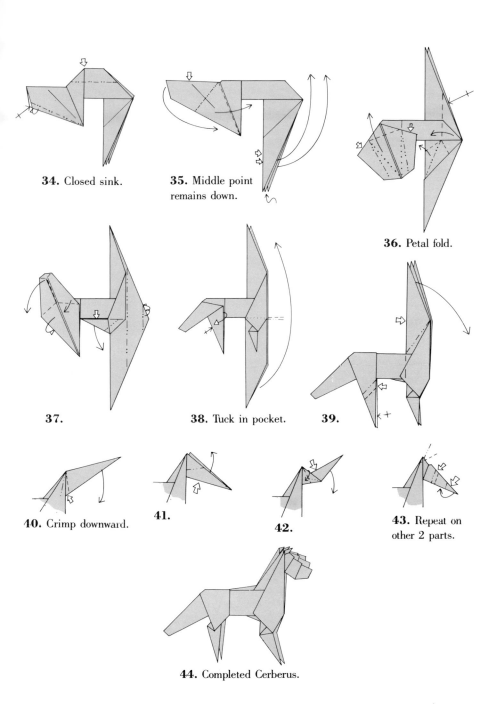

34. Closed sink.

35. Middle point remains down.

36. Petal fold.

37.

38. Tuck in pocket.

39.

40. Crimp downward.

41.

42.

43. Repeat on other 2 parts.

44. Completed Cerberus.

BIBLIOGRAPHY

Excellent, easy-to-find origami books:

Engel, Peter. *Folding the Universe*. New York: Vintage, 1989.

Kasahara, Kunihiko. *Creative Origami*. Tokyo: Japan Publications, 1967.

_____. *Origami Omnibus*. Tokyo: Japan Publications, 1988.

Kasahara, Kunihiko, and Toshie Takahama. *Origami for the Connoisseur*. Tokyo: Japan Publications, 1987.

Kennaway, Eric. *Complete Origami*. New York: St. Martin's Press, 1987.

Lang, Robert J. *The Complete Book of Origami*. New York: Dover, 1988.

Lang, Robert J., with John Montroll. *Origami Sea Life*. Vermont: Antroll, 1990.

Lang, Robert J., with Stephen Weiss. *Origami Zoo*. New York: St. Martin's Press, 1990.

Montroll, John. *Origami for the Enthusiast*. New York: Dover, 1979.

_____. *Animal Origami for the Enthusiast*. New York: Dover, 1985.

_____. *Origami Sculptures*. College Park, Maryland: Antroll, 1988.

_____. *Prehistoric Origami*. College Park, Maryland: Antroll, 1990.

Weiss, Stephen. *Wings and Things: Origami that Flies*. New York: St. Martin's Press, 1984.

Books on mythology and related subjects:

Bullfinch, Thomas. *Bullfinch's Mythology*. New York: Dell, 1959.

Campbell, Joseph. *The Hero With a Thousand Faces*. Princeton, NJ: Princeton University Press, 1949.

_____. *Creative Mythology*. New York: Penguin, 1968.

_____. *The Power of Myth*. New York: Doubleday, 1988.

Dickinson, Peter. *The Flight of Dragons*. New York: Harper and Row, 1979.

Fraser, Sir James. *The New Golden Bough*. New York: New American Library, 1959.

Graves, Robert. *The Greek Myths*. New York: Penguin, 1955.

––––––. *The White Goddess*. London: Faber and Faber, 1948.

Parrinder, Geoffrey. *World Religions: From Ancient History to the Present*. New York: Facts on File, 1971.

Williamson, Robin. *The Craneskin Bag*. Edinburgh: Cannongate, 1989.

SOURCES

Organizations

(Books and paper can also be ordered from origami societies. These groups are also wonderful resources for information on all aspects of paperfolding.)

The Friends of the
Origami Center of America
15 West 77 Street
Room ST-1
New York, NY 10024
(212) 769-5635

The British Origami Society
David Brill, General Secretary
253 Park Lane
Poynton, Stockport, Cheshire
SK12 1RH
United Kingdom
(0625) 8725 09

Supplies

Call or write to the following about their selection of papers produced expressly for origami and other distinctive papers that can be used for the craft.

Aiko's Art Materials Import, Inc.
3347 North Clark Street
Chicago, IL 60657
(312) 404-5600

Bunkado
340 East First Street
Los Angeles, CA 90012
(213) 625-8673

Five Eggs
436 West Broadway
New York, NY 10012
(212) 226-1606

The Japanese Paper Place
966 Queen Street West
Toronto, Ontario M6J IG8
Canada
(416) 533-6862

Kate's Paperie
8 West 13 Street
New York, NY 10011
(212) 633-0570

New York Central Art Supply
62 Third Avenue
New York, NY 10003
(212) 473-7705

The Paper Tree
1743 Buchanan Mall
San Francisco, CA 94115
(415) 921-7100

Taws
1527 Walnut Street
Philadelphia, PA 19102
(215) 563-8742

CREDITS

The following origami creators are represented in this book:
Gabriel Alvarez: Daedalus, page 39; Pegasus, page 44
Neal Elias: Centaur, page 59
Matthew Green: Long-tailed Dragon, page 81
Jerry Harris: Gargoyle, page 34
Mark Kirschenbaum: Rearing Dragon, page 64
Robert Lang: Shiva, page 70; Cerberus, page 88
Robert Neale: Ouroboros, page 22; Wizard and Witch, page 25; Winged
    Dragon, page 31
Stephen Weiss: Flapping Dragon, page 50; Woodland Elf, page 54;
    Unicorn, page 76